MACMILLAN
MUSIC and YOU

MVFOL

Barbara Staton, Senior Author
Merrill Staton, Senior Author
Marilyn Davidson
Susan Snyder

Macmillan Publishing Company
New York

Collier Macmillan Publishers
London

Cover Design and Illustration: Heather Cooper

Text Illustration: Randy Chewing, Len Ebert, Hima Pamoedjo, Jan Pyk, Lane Yerkes.

Photo Credits: CLARA AICH: 10B, 11TL, TR, 16, 17, 51. ART RESOURCE, NY: Scala, 42. THE BETTMANN ARCHIVE, INC.: 35. THE IMAGE BANK: © Robert Phillips, 10T. PHOTO RESEARCHERS, INC.: © Porterfield-Chickering, 45. THE PHOTO SOURCE: 20. PHOTOTAKE: © Yoav, 10C. VICTORIA BELLER SMITH: 4, 5, 23, 26B, 27T, 30, 36, 37, 39. MARTHA SWOPE PHOTOGRAPHY, INC.: 30B, 50. SUZANNE SZASZ: iv, 1, 26T, 27B.

Macmillan Publishing Company
866 Third Avenue
New York, N.Y. 10022
Collier Macmillan Canada, Inc.

Printed in the United States of America

ISBN: 0-02-293280-1   9 8

contents

We Make Music

You can use your voice four ways.

Listen

loud

soft

High and Low

HIGH

LOW

Steady Beat

Music Helps to Tell a Story

high

middle

7

Listening for Loud and Soft

bow wow

meow

quack quack

Long and Short

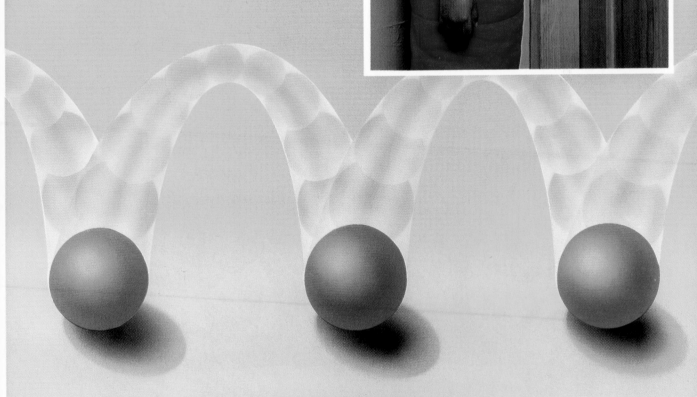

11

Playing High and Low

High

Low

Town Ball

What Sound Does Each Make?

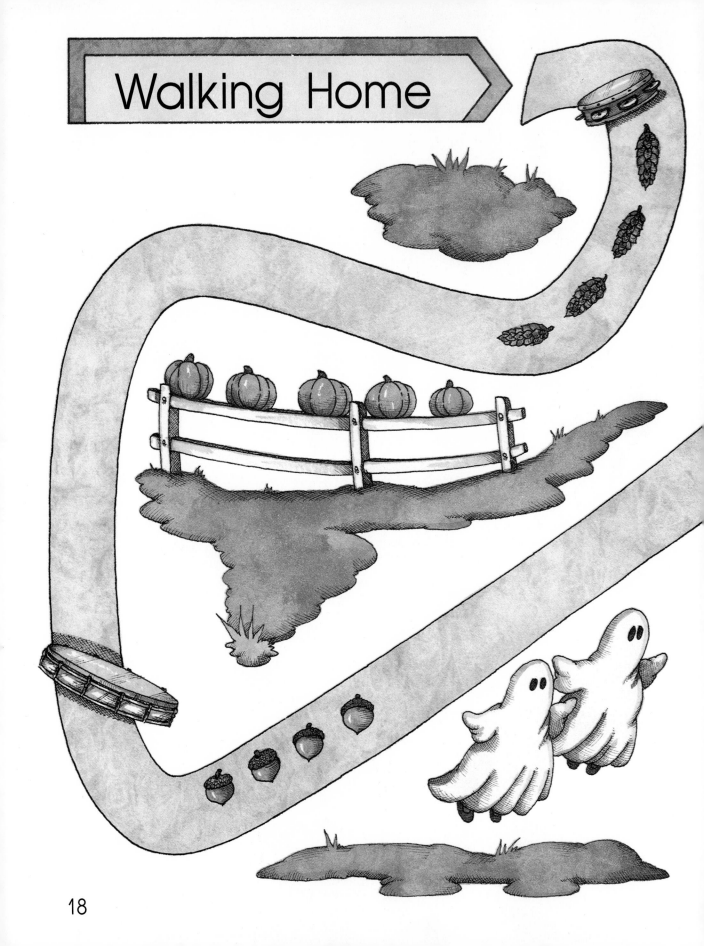

Walking Home

Look, Hear, and Move

Landscape With Cypresses. Vincent Van Gogh. Private Collection

Point the Beat

21

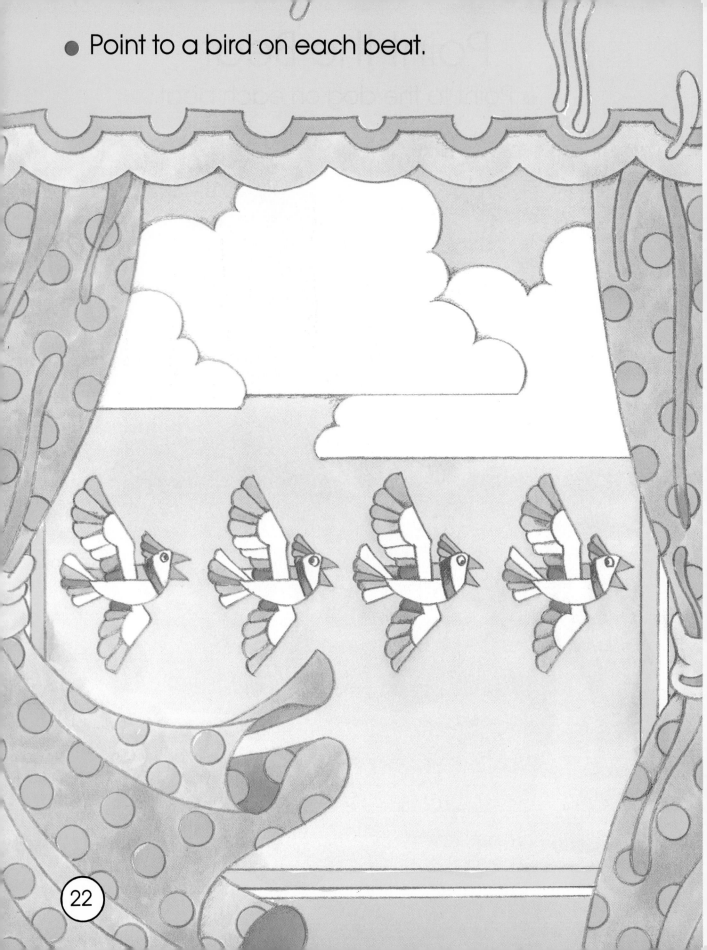

Play the Beat

● Play the beat.

Say It Fast and Slow

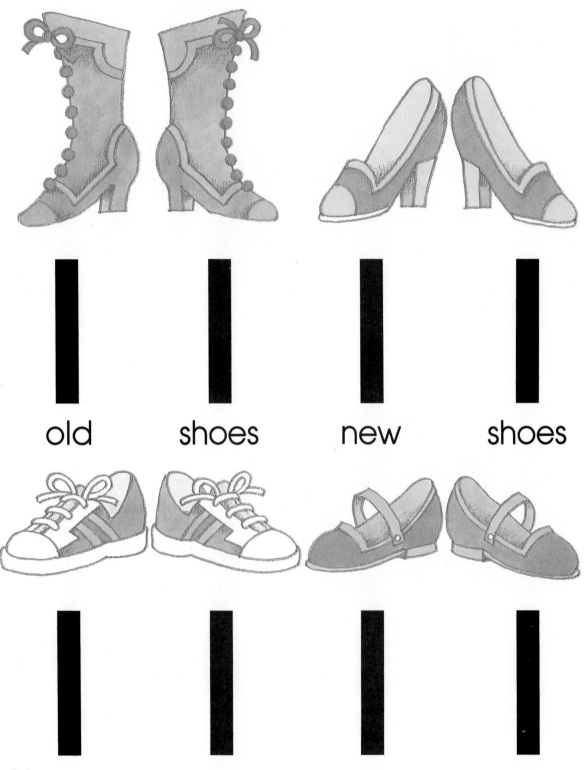

old   shoes   new   shoes

One Sound on Each Beat

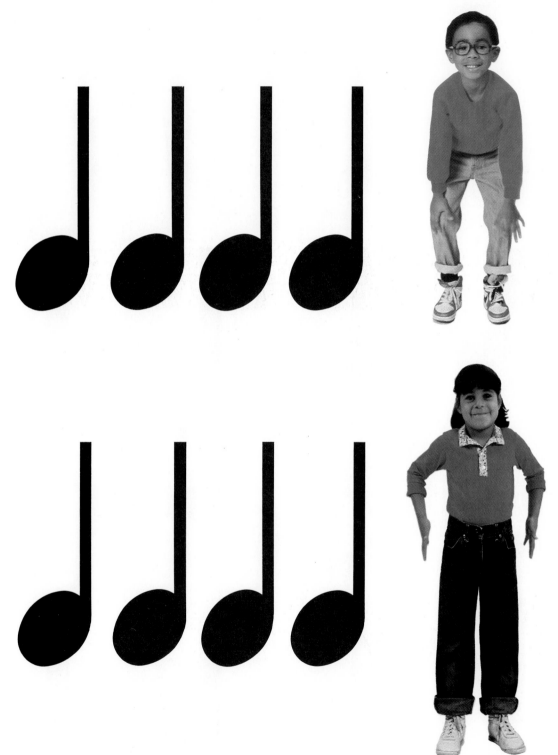

Same and Different

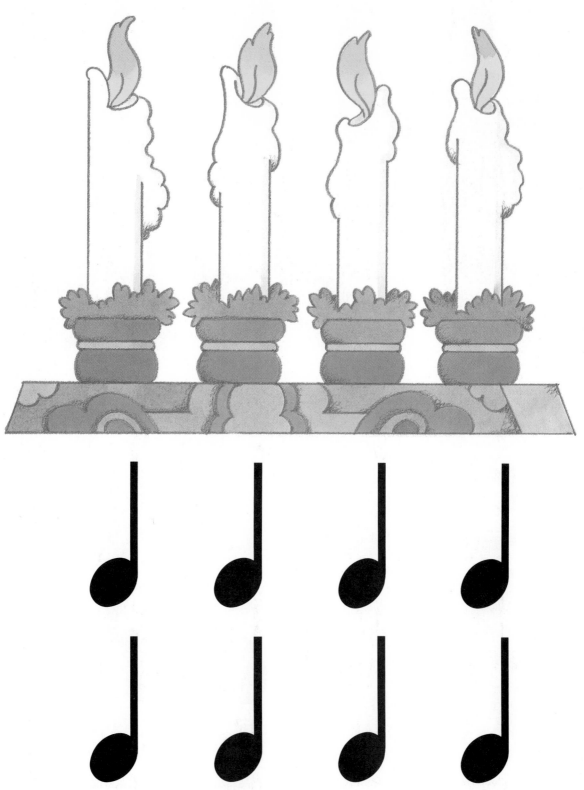

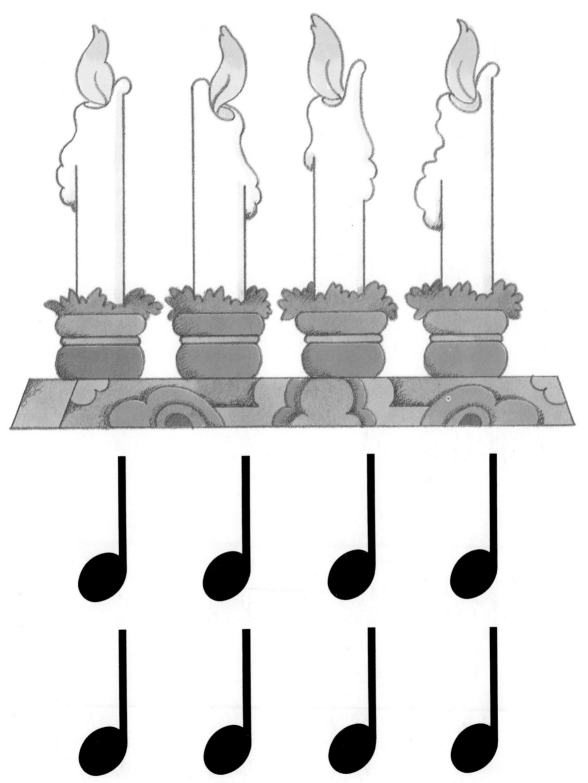

See what you hear.

piccolo   flute   cello   violin

Chinese Dance

Sound and
No Sound

Long and Short Sounds

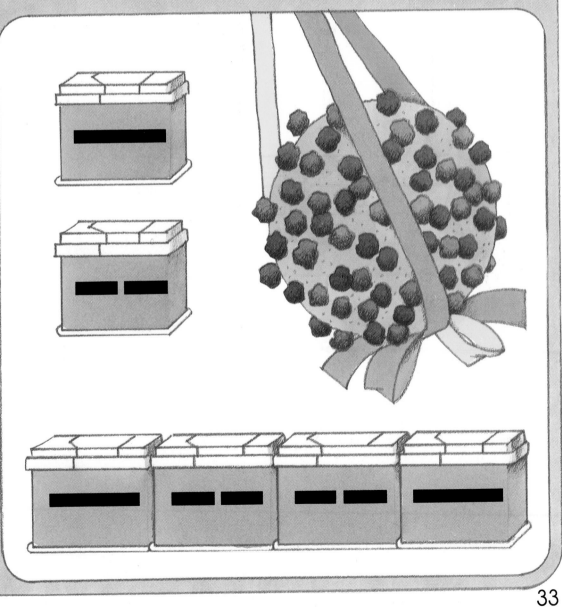

Picturing Sounds

so   mi   so   mi

Up on the Housetop

"Merry Christmas to All and to All a Goodnight," illustration to Clement Moore's
'Twas the Night Before Christmas, THE BETTMANN ARCHIVE, INC.

The Strong Beat

Pitches

The pitches stay the same.

Wake me

F

The pitches go down.

Gold - en   Gate

39

Peter and the Wolf

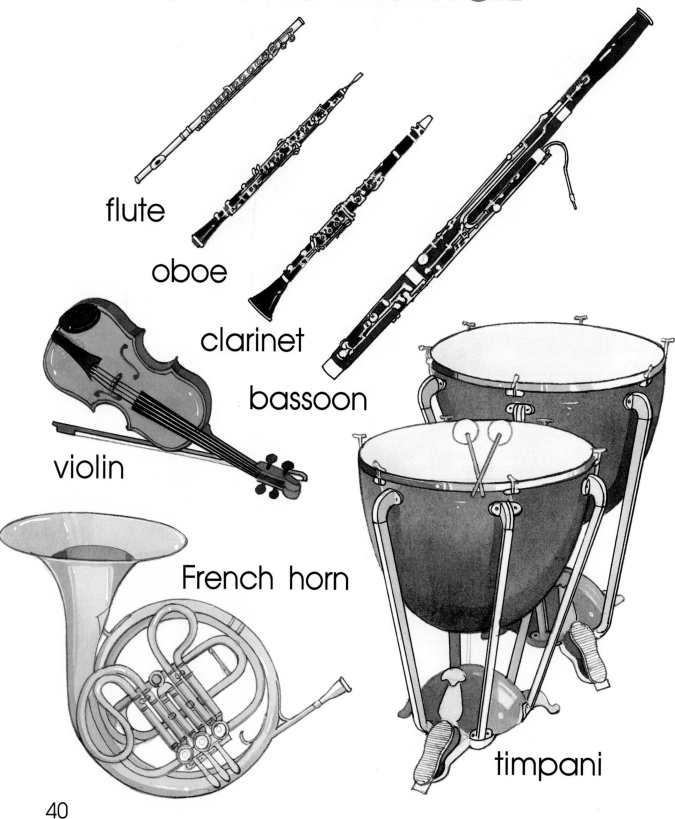

flute

oboe

clarinet

bassoon

violin

French horn

timpani

Two Sounds in a Beat

● Tap the rhythm.

Reading Rhythms

● Tap another rhythm.

hot   cold   old

● Find *la.*

so

Mes - sen - ger,   mes - sen - ger,

do   you   have   a   let - ter?

45

You can place notes.

More Rhythms to Read

- Say these rhythms.

- Say *friend* for ♩

- Say *happy* for ♫

- Say *bell* for ♩
- Say *horses* for ♫

Bell Horses

- Find *so.*
- Find *la.*

Beats in a Phrase

How many beats are in each **phrase?**

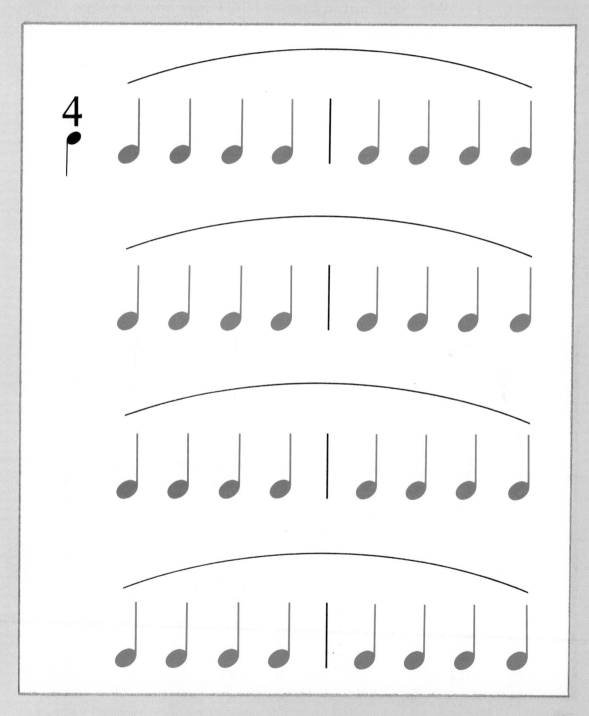

What Do You Hear?

Who will buy a broom here? Buy my brooms.

Which do you hear?

1.

2.

The Brass Family

- How are these the same?
- How are these different?

trumpet

trombone

tuba

French horn

Placing Pitches

When

so is in a space

mi is always in the space below *so*

and

la is always around the line above *so.*

When

so is around a line

mi is always around the line below *so*

and

la is always in the space above *so.*

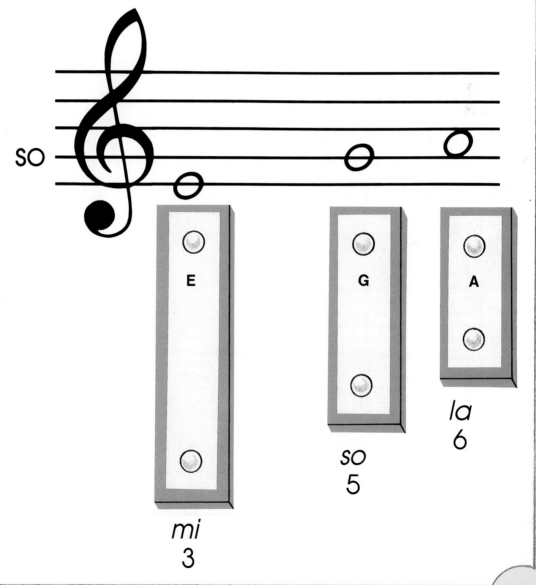

Rain Sounds

- Say *rain* for ♩
- Say *falling* for ♫

Rain, Rain Go Away

so Rain, rain, go a - way,

Come a - gain an - oth - er day.

Rain, rain, go a - way.

All the chil - dren want to play.

Sets of Beats

Beats can be in sets of two.

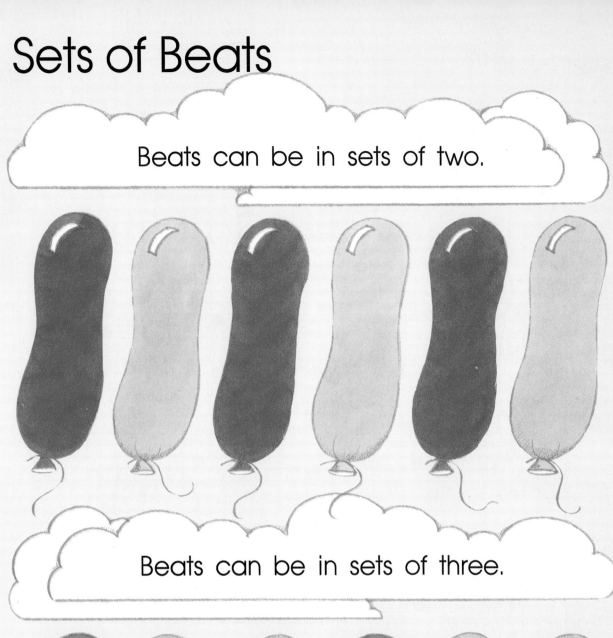

Beats can be in sets of three.

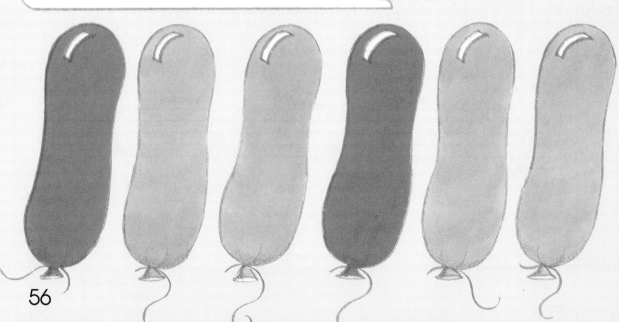

Form

Some music has two parts.

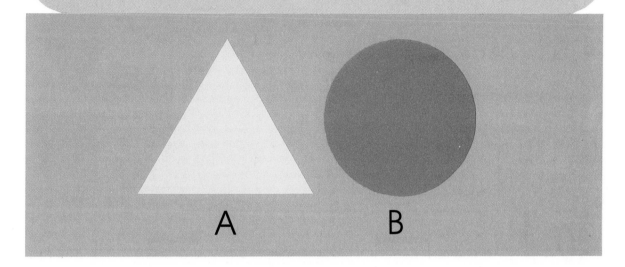

A   B

Some music has three parts.

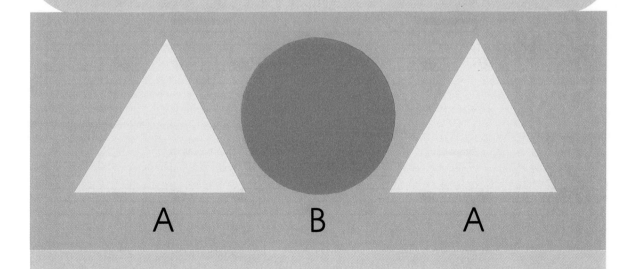

A   B   A

The order of the parts is called **form**.

Old and New Friends

- Read this song.
- Say *nine* for ♩
- Say *number* for ♫

Engine, Engine
Number Nine

- Count each *do* in this song.

How many can you find?

do — do mi so la
     1   3   5   6

Mouse Mousie

do

Mouse mous - ie, lit - tle mous - ie,

Hur - ry, hur - ry do!

Or the kit - ty in the hous - ie

Will be chas - ing you! (Run!)

59

Practice Rhythms
LOOSE TOOTH

I had a loose tooth, a wig-gly, jig-gly loose tooth,

I had a loose tooth, hang-ing by a thread.

So I pulled my loose tooth, this wig-gly, jig-gly loose tooth, And

put it 'neath my pil-low and then I went to bed. The

fair-ies took my loose tooth, my wig-gly, jig-gly loose tooth, So

now I have a quar-ter and a hole in my head.

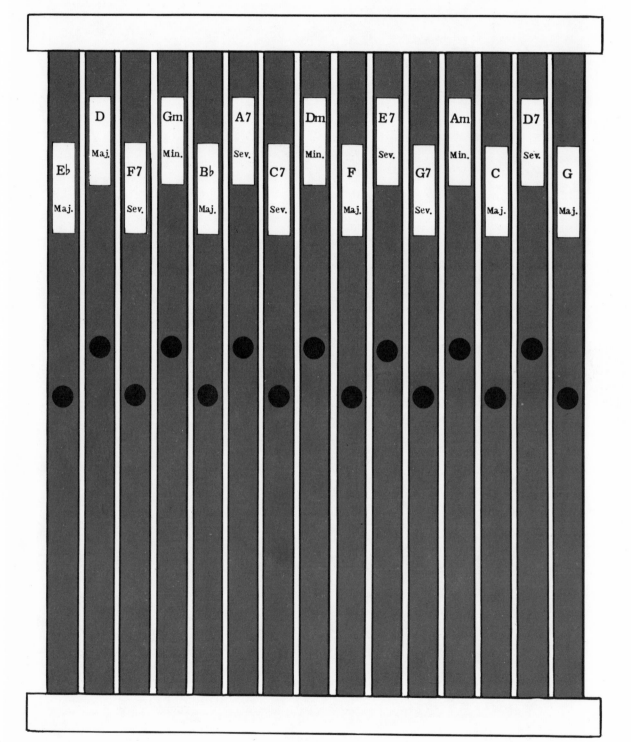